Table of Contents

1 Introduction to Cybercrime

Cybercrime, in its simplest form, is illegal activity committed using a computer or network. It's not just about hacking; it encompasses a broad spectrum of offenses, from stealing financial information to spreading malicious software and disrupting essential services. The core element is the exploitation of digital technology for illicit gain or malicious intent. This differs significantly from traditional crime, which primarily operates within the physical world. Cybercrime's borderless nature makes it exceptionally challenging to investigate and prosecute, requiring international collaboration and innovative approaches to law enforcement.

Unlike a physical bank robbery, a cyberattack can be launched from anywhere in the world, targeting victims across continents. The anonymity afforded by the internet makes identifying perpetrators difficult, often leading to protracted investigations and complex legal proceedings. Jurisdictional issues further complicate matters, as determining which legal system applies can be challenging when offenses transcend national borders. Consequently, prosecuting cybercriminals often requires intricate international cooperation and a deep understanding of diverse legal frameworks. The constantly evolving technological landscape also necessitates continuous adaptation in legal strategies and enforcement methods.

Many factors motivate cybercriminals. Financial gain is a primary driver, with the potential for significant profits from activities like credit card fraud and ransomware attacks. Some are driven by political ideology, seeking to disrupt systems or spread propaganda. Others engage in cybercrime for personal gratification, such as defacing websites or conducting denial-of-service attacks. The motivations are diverse, but the underlying commonality is the exploitation of technological vulnerabilities for illegitimate purposes. Understanding these motivations is critical in developing effective prevention strategies and targeted interventions.

The scale of cybercrime is immense and growing exponentially. Millions of individuals and organizations are affected annually, suffering financial losses, data breaches, and reputational damage. The economic impact is staggering, with costs ranging from lost productivity to the expenses incurred in recovering from attacks. This financial burden extends beyond the direct victims, affecting insurance companies, government agencies, and the broader economy. The sheer scale of the problem necessitates comprehensive strategies involving technological advancements, regulatory frameworks, and public awareness campaigns to combat its pervasive impact.

Cybercrime's effects ripple far beyond immediate financial losses. Data breaches can lead to identity theft, exposing personal information to malicious actors. The emotional distress caused by such violations can be profound and long-lasting, impacting mental health and overall well-being. Reputational damage to organizations following a cyberattack can significantly impact their business, hindering future growth and investor confidence. Furthermore, critical infrastructure attacks can have devastating consequences, disrupting essential services like power grids, transportation systems, and healthcare facilities, posing significant risks to public safety and so-

cietal stability.
Consider the case of a seemingly harmless phishing email. It might appear to be from a legitimate source, prompting the recipient to reveal sensitive information, such as banking details or login credentials. This seemingly small interaction can trigger a chain reaction leading to significant financial losses and identity theft. The attacker, operating remotely and anonymously, exploits human psychology to gain access to valuable information, highlighting the crucial role of human factors in cybercrime. This vulnerability underlines the need for effective cybersecurity education and training.
Therefore, understanding cybercrime is not merely an academic exercise; it's a crucial skill for navigating the increasingly digital world. It necessitates a multifaceted approach, combining technological expertise with an understanding of legal frameworks, ethical considerations, and the complexities of human behavior. A robust defense against cybercrime relies not only on strong technological safeguards but also on informed users who can recognize and avoid social engineering tactics. The future of cybersecurity requires a concerted effort across various disciplines and sectors.
The consequences of a successful cyberattack can be devastating. Imagine a hospital system crippled by ransomware, unable to access patient records or administer vital care. Or consider a financial institution facing a massive data breach, exposing the personal information of millions of customers. The implications extend far beyond simple financial loss; they affect public health, national security, and trust in digital institutions. This underscores the importance of proactive security measures and effective crisis management plans.
This introduction has set the stage for a deeper dive into the various forms of cybercrime, their underlying mechanisms, and the strategies used to combat them. The subsequent chapters will ex-

plore the mathematical underpinnings of cryptographic vulnerabilities, network intrusion detection techniques, data hiding methods, and financial fraud schemes. We will also delve into the psychology of social engineering and the legal and ethical considerations surrounding cybercrime. Understanding the intricacies of cybercrime requires a multidisciplinary perspective, bridging computer science, mathematics, law, and psychology. This knowledge forms the bedrock for protecting ourselves in the digital age.

1.1 Defining Cybercrime

Cybercrime, in its simplest definition, involves any illegal activity that uses a computer or network as its primary tool or target. It's not just about sophisticated hacking; it encompasses a vast spectrum of criminal enterprises, ranging from petty theft to large-scale organized crime. The key difference between cybercrime and traditional crime lies in the utilization of digital infrastructure—the internet, computer systems, and mobile devices—as essential components of the crime's commission or impact. This digital aspect introduces unique challenges in terms of investigation, prosecution, and prevention, demanding specialized expertise and interdisciplinary collaboration.

Unlike robbing a bank, which leaves clear physical evidence, many cybercrimes leave behind only digital footprints, often scattered across multiple jurisdictions and systems. Tracing these digital trails requires advanced technical skills, a thorough understanding of network protocols, and often, international cooperation. Furthermore, the anonymity offered by the internet makes identifying and apprehending perpetrators exceedingly difficult, necessitating innovative investigative techniques and persistent effort. Consider the challenges presented by distributed denial-of-service attacks (DDoS), where the source of the attack is masked by a network of compromised computers around the globe. Tracking down the perpetrators in such a case requires sophisticated forensic analysis and a detailed understanding of the attack's infrastructure.

The rapid evolution of technology presents another significant hurdle. Cybercriminals constantly adapt their methods, exploiting emerging vulnerabilities and developing new techniques to bypass security measures. This constant arms race between criminals and law enforcement agencies is a defining feature of the cybercrime landscape, requiring a continuous cycle of learning, innovation, and adaptation. The use of encryption, for instance, can both protect legitimate data and shield criminal activities, highlighting the double-edged sword of technological advancements. Effective cybersecurity strategies must therefore strike a balance between security and usability, avoiding excessively restrictive measures that impede daily operations.

Moreover, the impact of cybercrime extends far beyond monetary losses. The theft of personal data, such as social security numbers, credit card information, or medical records, can have devastating consequences for individuals. Identity theft, often a component of larger cybercrime schemes, can cripple credit ratings, damage reputations, and result in substantial financial burdens. Beyond individuals, corporations and governments are also vulnerable, facing disruptions to operations, financial losses, and reputational damage. A successful cyberattack against a critical infrastructure system, such as a power grid or financial institution, could have catastrophic effects, underscoring the importance of robust cybersecurity measures.

Defining specific types of cybercrime further highlights the complexity. Hacking, perhaps the most recognizable form, ranges from unauthorized access to systems for personal gain to large-scale data breaches targeting sensitive information. Malware, encompassing viruses, worms, and ransomware, presents another major threat, capable of crippling systems, stealing data, or demanding ransom payments. Financial crimes, like online fraud and phishing scams, exploit the trust placed in online transactions to steal money or personal information. These examples only scratch the surface of the multifaceted nature of cybercrime. Understanding these varied forms is crucial to developing comprehensive prevention and mitigation strategies. The constantly evolving nature of cybercrime necessitates a continuous update of our understanding and a proactive approach to protecting ourselves and our data. The boundaries of cybercrime are constantly shifting, necessitating a dynamic and adaptive response from law enforcement, businesses, and individuals alike. It is a battle fought in the digital shadows, and understanding its nuances is the first step toward combating it.

The pervasiveness and constantly shifting nature of cybercrime require a multi-faceted approach to its study and prevention. The legal and ethical dimensions are critical; understanding the relevant laws and the ethical implications of cyber activity forms a cornerstone of responsible engagement with the digital world. The development of sophisticated cybersecurity measures, encompassing network security, data protection, and incident response planning, is paramount. Furthermore, a profound understanding of the mathematical principles underlying cryptography and data security is crucial for effectively defending against sophisticated cyberattacks. Education and awareness are equally important, empowering individuals to recognize and avoid becoming victims of cybercrime. This complex web of technical, legal, and ethical considerations underscores the multifaceted nature of this growing global challenge. The pursuit of solutions necessitates a collaborative effort from various stakeholders to create a more secure and responsible digital environment.

1.2 Types of Cybercrime

Cybercrime manifests in diverse forms, each employing unique methods and targeting various vulnerabilities. Understanding these distinctions is crucial for effective prevention and mitigation. Categorizing these crimes allows for a more focused approach to security strategies.

One prevalent category is malware distribution, encompassing viruses, worms, trojans, and ransomware. These malicious software programs infiltrate systems, often through deceptive downloads or email attachments. Viruses replicate themselves, spreading across networks, while worms exploit security flaws to self-propagate. Trojans disguise themselves as legitimate software, granting attackers unauthorized access. Ransomware encrypts data, demanding payment for its release. The sophistication of these attacks is constantly evolving, requiring continuous updates to antivirus software and robust security protocols. The financial implications for individuals and organizations can be devastating, leading to data loss, system downtime, and significant monetary expenses. Moreover, the recovery process can be lengthy and complex, often requiring specialized expertise. Prevention involves education on safe browsing practices, regular software updates, and robust endpoint protection.

Another significant category involves hacking, the unauthorized access and manipulation of computer systems. This can range from simple attacks targeting individual accounts to sophisticated intrusions targeting large organizations, or even governmental infrastructure. Hackers employ various techniques, from exploiting software vulnerabilities to using social engineering tactics to gain access. The motivations behind these attacks can vary, from financial gain to data theft, espionage, or simply the thrill of the challenge. The consequences, however, are consistently severe. Data breaches can expose sensitive personal or financial information, leading to identity theft, financial losses, and reputational damage. Network disruptions can cause significant downtime and financial losses for businesses and organizations. Furthermore, the impact extends beyond immediate losses, often leading to long-term recovery efforts and legal consequences. A strong defense requires robust network security measures, regular security audits, and employee training on cybersecurity best practices.

Financial crimes represent another significant area. These often involve online fraud schemes, exploiting vulnerabilities in online banking systems and financial transactions. Credit card fraud, for instance, involves stealing credit card information through phishing attacks or malware infections. Online banking attacks frequently leverage malware to steal login credentials or intercept transactions. These attacks can lead to significant financial losses for individuals and businesses, as well as reputational damage and legal ramifications. Prevention involves the use of strong passwords, multi-factor authentication, and regular monitoring of bank statements. Staying informed about emerging threats and fraud tactics is equally vital. The complexity of these crimes frequently necessitates collaboration between law enforcement agencies and financial institutions.

Identity theft is a particularly insidious form of cybercrime, where criminals steal personal information such as names, Social Security numbers, or credit card details to assume the victim's identity. This theft is often achieved through phishing scams, data breaches, or malware infections. The long-term consequences of identity theft can be devastating, extending to damaged credit scores, financial losses, and the difficult process of restoring one's identity. Combating this necessitates both individual precautions, like password management and fraud monitoring, and broader efforts involving data protection legislation and responsible data handling practices by organizations. The multifaceted nature of this crime underlines the need for a holistic, multi-layered approach to prevention and remediation.

Denial-of-service (DoS) attacks represent yet another crucial type of cybercrime. These attacks flood a target system with traffic, rendering it unavailable to legitimate users. This can cripple online businesses, disrupt governmental services, and even affect critical infrastructure. Distributed Denial-of-Service (DDoS) attacks, using multiple compromised systems to launch the assault, are particularly effective and challenging to defend against. Mitigation strategies involve implementing robust network infrastructure, utilizing content delivery networks, and having effective incident response plans. These attacks highlight the interconnectedness of modern systems and the need for robust defenses against large-scale attacks. The impact extends far beyond mere inconvenience; it can affect countless users, disrupt critical services, and result in significant financial losses. The persistent evolution of DoS techniques necessitates ongoing adaptation in defensive strategies.

2 Cryptographic Vulnerabilities

Weak encryption, a seemingly simple concept, represents a significant vulnerability. Criminals can exploit outdated or poorly implemented encryption algorithms to easily access sensitive data. Imagine a digital fortress built with flimsy wood instead of reinforced concrete; that's the effect of weak encryption. The consequences can range from minor inconveniences like unauthorized access to email accounts to catastrophic breaches exposing highly sensitive personal or financial information. The use of outdated standards like DES or weak key sizes in AES dramatically increases the risk. Updating to stronger, more modern algorithms and employing sufficient key lengths is paramount; a seemingly small change can drastically bolster your security. This underscores the importance of regular security audits and proactive updates to protect against these easily exploitable weaknesses.

Key management is another critical area. Even with strong encryption, vulnerabilities arise if keys are poorly managed. This involves everything from the generation and storage of keys to their distribution and revocation. A compromised key renders even the strongest encryption useless. Consider a scenario where a company uses the same key across multiple systems—if one system is compromised, the entire network is vulnerable. Secure key management protocols, including rigorous access controls, regular key rotation, and the use of hardware security modules (HSMs) are essential. Robust protocols are not just about the technology; a crucial element is human training. Employees must be thoroughly educated on safe key handling practices, understanding the gravity of even seemingly small mistakes. Negligence in this area can have devastating consequences, costing businesses millions in damages and causing irreparable damage to reputation.

Side-channel attacks represent a more subtle but equally dangerous threat. These attacks exploit unintentional information leaks during cryptographic operations, not by directly breaking the encryption algorithm, but by observing ancillary data. Imagine a spy listening to the sounds from inside a room rather than trying to pick its lock. This could reveal timing variations in encryption processes or power consumption patterns, which reveal information about the processed data or cryptographic key. Examples include timing attacks and power analysis. Mitigating these attacks requires careful design and implementation of cryptographic systems, taking into account potential side channels. This involves the use of countermeasures like constant-time algorithms and techniques to randomize operations and mask sensitive information. Understanding the various types of side-channel attacks and implementing appropriate defenses is crucial for building robust and resilient cryptographic systems. The complexity here highlights the need for specialized expertise in cryptographic engineering, rather than simple implementation. A thorough understanding of the underlying hardware and software is crucial to detect and prevent these attacks effectively. This often requires collaboration across different departments and a multi-faceted approach rather than simple reliance on a singular technique.

The implications of cryptographic vulnerabilities are far-reaching. They affect not only individuals but also organizations and governments, leading to data breaches, financial losses, reputational damage, and legal ramifications. In a connected world, where information is the lifeblood of commerce and governance, the security of data is paramount. Ignoring or underestimating these vulnerabilities can have severe consequences. Therefore, a strong understanding of cryptographic principles and the practical application of secure practices is no longer a luxury but a necessity in today's digital landscape. Proactive measures, regular audits and a commitment to security best practices are essential to maintain a secure environment. Ultimately, strengthening our defenses against these vulnerabilities requires a multifaceted approach encompassing strong encryption, robust key management, and effective defenses against side-channel attacks. This involves a combination of technological solutions, rigorous policies, and comprehensive security awareness training for all stakeholders. Investing in security is not just a cost, it's an investment in the protection of critical assets. The consequences of ignoring these vulnerabilities far outweigh the costs of implementing robust security measures.

2.1 Weak Encryption

Weak encryption, at its core, represents a significant vulnerability in the digital landscape. It's not simply about using outdated algorithms; it's about a fundamental misunderstanding of the principles underlying strong cryptography. A poorly chosen cipher, a short key length, or an implementation riddled with flaws can all drastically reduce the security provided, leaving sensitive data exposed to determined attackers. Consider the difference between a flimsy padlock and a high-security deadbolt – the former offers little resistance, while the latter requires specialized tools and considerable effort to breach. Similarly, weak encryption is easily cracked, often with readily available tools and minimal expertise.

The consequences of weak encryption are far-reaching and potentially devastating. Imagine a company using an outdated encryption algorithm to protect customer credit card details. A successful attack could lead to widespread identity theft and financial losses, not only for the individuals affected but also for the company's reputation and bottom line. This sort of breach can expose personal identifiable information (PII), leading to severe consequences that extend beyond simple financial theft. It's a cascading effect. The initial compromise could expose medical records, social security numbers, or even intellectual property. Legal ramifications and hefty fines will follow. Furthermore, such events deeply erode public trust in the affected institution.

Understanding the mechanics of weak encryption requires a closer look at cryptographic algorithms themselves. Symmetric encryption, relying on a single key for both encryption and decryption, becomes highly vulnerable with weak key sizes. A 64-bit key, for instance, is far too short in the current computational environment; brute-force attacks can quickly uncover the key. Asymmetric encryption, though conceptually stronger due to its use of public and private key pairs, suffers from vulnerabilities when the mathematical underpinnings are weak or poorly implemented. RSA, a widely used public-key cryptosystem, is prone to attack if the key generation process is flawed or if the modulus is too small. These vulnerabilities create avenues for attackers to decipher encrypted messages and gain unauthorized access to sensitive data.

Moreover, the weaknesses are not solely limited to the algorithms themselves. Implementation flaws can severely compromise the security provided by even strong algorithms. Improper handling of random number generators, for instance, can lead to predictable keys. Side-channel attacks, such as timing analysis or power consumption monitoring, can exploit subtle variations in the encryption process to deduce information about the key. Even seemingly minor coding errors, or bugs, can provide an attacker a foothold to exploit the system and compromise its integrity. This means that robust encryption isn't just about selecting a secure algorithm; it's also about careful and secure implementation.

The choice of encryption algorithm should always align with the sensitivity of the data being protected. For high-value assets, such as financial transactions or health records, only the strongest, most vetted algorithms should be used, employing appropriate key sizes and robust implementation practices. Regular security audits and penetration testing are crucial for detecting potential vulnerabilities. Remember that security is an ongoing process, not a one-time fix. Staying up-to-date on the latest cryptographic advances and regularly updating software and hardware are vital components of comprehensive cybersecurity. Neglecting these precautions increases your vulnerability exponentially. The consequences of complacency can be severe.

To strengthen your defenses against attacks leveraging weak encryption, adopt a multi-layered approach. Combine strong encryption with other security measures, such as access controls, intrusion detection systems, and regular security audits. This layered approach makes it significantly harder for attackers to penetrate your defenses, even if one layer is compromised. Employee training is also crucial. Educating staff about phishing attacks and social engineering tactics reduces the likelihood of human error compromising the system.

Remember that the weakest link is often the human element.
Finally, understanding the limitations of any security measure is paramount. No system is completely impenetrable. However, by employing strong encryption practices and a layered security approach, you can significantly reduce the risk of cyberattacks and protect your valuable data. The cost of neglecting these precautions vastly outweighs the investment in time and resources required for their implementation. Proactive security measures, rather than reactive ones, are far more effective and efficient. In short, selecting the right encryption and understanding its vulnerabilities are key to safeguarding your data.

2.2 Key Management Issues

Secure key management is paramount; neglecting it invites catastrophe. A compromised key is a compromised system, regardless of the sophistication of the encryption algorithm itself. Think of it like a fortress with a flimsy gate – the strongest walls mean nothing if the entry point is weak. Robust key management isn't just about generating strong keys; it's about the entire lifecycle, from creation to destruction. This involves carefully considering generation methods, storage protocols, access control mechanisms, and ultimately, secure key destruction. Ignoring any of these aspects risks catastrophic security breaches.
Key generation itself needs meticulous attention. Randomness is crucial; a predictable key is easily broken. Many algorithms exist, but their strength depends on the quality of the random number generator (RNG) employed. Weak RNGs, often found in poorly designed systems, yield predictable keys, rendering encryption useless. Cryptographically secure pseudo-random number generators

(CSPRNGs) are essential for producing keys with sufficient entropy, ensuring their unpredictability. Furthermore, the length of the key is vital; longer keys offer significantly increased resistance to brute-force attacks. The choice of key length should align with the sensitivity of the data and the expected lifespan of the security system. Failing to use a suitable CSPRNG or an adequate key length drastically weakens the cryptographic system's security.

Storage is another crucial phase often overlooked. Keys stored insecurely are vulnerable to theft, regardless of their strength. Storing keys directly on the device they protect creates an enormous risk. A compromised device gives immediate access to the key. Instead, consider hardware security modules (HSMs) or other physically secure devices for key storage. These provide a tamper-resistant environment, protecting keys even if the main system is breached. Another option is key splitting, distributing key components across multiple secure locations to prevent single points of failure. No matter the chosen approach, the security of the storage system is undeniably crucial; a breached storage system means a compromised key.

Access control is the next line of defense. Strict procedures are required to govern who can access keys. The principle of least privilege should be strictly enforced, limiting access to only those individuals and systems legitimately needing it. Multi-factor authentication (MFA), incorporating factors like something you know (password), something you have (token), and something you are (biometrics), significantly enhances security. Regular audits of access logs help identify potential unauthorized access attempts. Failing to implement and actively monitor proper access control can lead to catastrophic data loss.

Finally, key destruction is often neglected but is just as critical as creation and storage. When keys are no longer needed, they must be securely erased. Simple deletion isn't sufficient; the data might be recoverable. Secure deletion methods, employing techniques like overwriting or physical destruction, ensure complete data removal. Implementing a clear key lifecycle policy, specifying key generation, usage, storage, and secure destruction procedures, is essential for creating a robust security posture. It prevents accidental or malicious key compromise and unauthorized access.

Failing to implement rigorous key management practices leaves systems susceptible to a wide range of attacks. From simple brute-force attempts to sophisticated side-channel attacks, vulnerabilities in key management are frequently exploited by cybercriminals. Strong keys are only as good as the systems protecting them. A comprehensive key management strategy, encompassing all aspects of the key lifecycle, is fundamental to building robust cryptographic systems and safeguarding sensitive data. This chapter emphasizes that secure key management is not a singular task but a continuous process requiring vigilance and adherence to best practices throughout. Overlooking any one facet can render an otherwise secure system vulnerable to crippling attacks, leading to significant data breaches and potentially immense financial and reputational losses. Therefore, implementing and meticulously maintaining these practices are paramount for safeguarding sensitive information in today's digital landscape. The consequences of neglecting these crucial aspects can be severe, leading to breaches, data losses, financial damage, and damage to an organization's reputation.

2.3 Side-Channel Attacks

Side-channel attacks exploit information leaked during cryptographic operations, bypassing the intended security mechanisms.

Instead of directly attacking the encryption algorithm itself, these attacks focus on observing physical characteristics of the system performing the cryptography, such as power consumption, timing variations, or electromagnetic emissions. Think of it like eavesdropping not on the conversation itself, but on the subtle noises around the speakers—a cough, a whispered aside, the rustle of papers—these seemingly insignificant details can reveal crucial secrets. Consider a scenario involving a smart card, a tiny computer often used for secure authentication. While performing a cryptographic operation, the card might consume slightly more or less power depending on the specific data being processed. A sophisticated attacker could monitor this power consumption using specialized equipment, carefully analyzing the fluctuations. These minute variations, imperceptible to the naked eye, might reveal patterns correlated with the secret cryptographic key, effectively compromising the card's security without ever directly accessing the encryption algorithm itself. This is a prime example of a power analysis side-channel attack.

Timing attacks represent another insidious class of side-channel attacks. They focus on the time taken to complete a cryptographic operation. Even minor variations in execution time can leak information about the processed data. This type of attack frequently exploits conditional branches in the cryptographic algorithm's code. If the execution time changes based on the value of a secret key bit, an attacker can infer the key bit by measuring these time variations repeatedly. The attacker might send many requests, each time carefully measuring the response time, and then statistically analyze the results to recover the key. Precision is key; minute differences across many attempts provide sufficient information.

Electromagnetic (EM) emanations are another avenue for side-channel attacks. All electronic devices emit electromagnetic radiation as a byproduct of their operation. This radiation can contain information that reveals internal states and operations. Sophisticated attackers can use specialized EM probes to intercept this radiation, and then analyze it for signals correlated to the cryptographic operations being performed. The intercepted signals might reveal the key or other sensitive data. This type of attack requires advanced equipment and technical expertise, making it more sophisticated but also potentially more devastating.

The impact of these attacks extends far beyond simple data breaches. Compromising a cryptographic system through a side-channel attack can have devastating consequences for individuals and organizations. Financial institutions might face massive fraud, confidential government data could fall into the wrong hands, and critical infrastructure systems could be paralyzed. Understanding these attacks is vital for developing robust security measures.

Mitigation strategies against side-channel attacks require a multilayered approach. One important strategy is the use of countermeasures within the cryptographic implementation itself. These countermeasures aim to mask the correlation between the processed data and the observable side-channel characteristics. Techniques like masking and blinding randomly alter the data being processed during the cryptographic operation, making it difficult for an attacker to observe any clear correlations.

Another important strategy involves minimizing the information leaked through side channels. This can be achieved through careful hardware design, choosing less vulnerable cryptographic algorithms, and minimizing the amount of time the system spends processing sensitive data. Regular software updates can also play a critical role, patching known vulnerabilities and incorporating the latest security improvements. Careful physical security is also crucial, limiting access to equipment that might be used to monitor side channels.

Finally, building awareness is essential. Educating developers and security professionals about the nature and impact of side-channel attacks is crucial in mitigating their threat. By understanding how these attacks work and what countermeasures are available, we can build more secure systems. Remember, even seemingly insignificant details can be exploited. Thorough understanding of these attacks, coupled with proactive mitigation strategies, can significantly strengthen the security of our cryptographic systems against these insidious threats, protecting sensitive data and thwarting malicious activities. The defense against these covert calculations requires constant vigilance and an understanding of their subtle techniques. The fight for secure communication and data protection demands that we remain one step ahead of those who seek to exploit the weaknesses in our technology.

3 Network Intrusion Detection

Network intrusion detection systems (NIDS) are crucial for safeguarding computer networks. They act as sentinels, constantly monitoring network traffic for suspicious patterns and unauthorized access attempts. Think of them as the security guards of the digital world, tirelessly scanning for intruders. Effective NIDS implementation requires a comprehensive understanding of various techniques and their limitations. A poorly implemented system might miss critical threats or generate excessive false positives, rendering it ineffective. Successful deployment depends on understanding both the network's specific needs and the strengths and weaknesses of the available technologies. This understanding is paramount for choosing appropriate tools and establishing effective security protocols. It's about knowing what to look for and how to interpret the results.

Signature-based intrusion detection systems, a common approach, rely on pre-defined signatures – essentially fingerprints of known malicious activities. When the system encounters network traffic matching a signature, it flags it as potentially malicious. This method is effective against known attacks, offering a quick and reliable detection mechanism. However, signature-based systems struggle with zero-day exploits – novel attacks that haven't yet been identified and thus lack a corresponding signature in the system's database. This limitation underscores the importance of staying updated with the latest threat intelligence and regularly updating the signature database. Failure to do so leaves the network vulnerable to these unknown threats. The process of constantly updating the signatures is vital and often overlooked.

Anomaly detection, in contrast, takes a more proactive approach. It establishes a baseline of "normal" network behavior and flags deviations from this baseline as potential intrusions. This method doesn't rely on pre-defined signatures, making it inherently more adaptable to zero-day attacks. The process involves analyzing various network parameters such as traffic volume, frequency, and data types. Significant deviations from the established norms trigger alerts, signaling potential malicious activities. However, accurately defining what constitutes "normal" behavior can be challenging, and defining the threshold of what is an anomaly is very important. Misinterpreting normal fluctuations as malicious activity leads to high numbers of false positives, potentially overwhelming system administrators and reducing the system's overall effectiveness. The creation of robust algorithms for anomaly detection remains an active area of research.

Implementing effective NIDS involves a multi-faceted approach. Proper network segmentation is crucial, creating isolated zones to limit the impact of a breach. This approach helps contain the damage and prevents the spread of malware throughout the entire network. Intrusion detection systems should be strategically placed within the network to monitor critical areas. Regular system updates are essential to patch known vulnerabilities, preventing attackers from exploiting weaknesses to compromise the network. Furthermore, regular security audits are vital. These audits help evaluate the overall effectiveness of the NIDS and identify areas for improvement. They are a feedback mechanism ensuring the system remains effective against evolving threats.

The choice between signature-based and anomaly-based detection often involves a balance. Many modern systems integrate both methods, combining the strengths of each approach. Signature-based detection provides immediate identification of known threats, while anomaly detection offers broader protection against novel attacks. This hybrid approach significantly strengthens the network's defense capabilities, enabling it to effectively detect and respond to a wider range of attacks. Proper configuration and maintenance are essential to maximize the effectiveness of any chosen system. Regular monitoring of system logs and alerts is crucial to quickly identify and respond to any suspicious activity. The speed and accuracy of this response are critical in minimizing the impact of potential attacks.

Successfully deploying and managing a robust NIDS requires a blend of technical skills, strategic thinking, and awareness of the ever-evolving threat landscape. It's not merely about installing software; it's about understanding the intricate dance between attackers and defenders, and constantly adapting to stay ahead of the curve. The continuous learning aspect of this field is paramount – constantly updating knowledge of new techniques, evolving threats, and improving the system's efficacy. This involves a constant feedback loop of monitoring, analyzing, and adapting the system to stay ahead of potential intrusions. In the end, a robust NIDS is more than just technology; it's a dynamic strategy, constantly evolving to protect valuable network resources.

3.1 Anomaly Detection

Anomaly detection in network security relies on identifying deviations from established patterns. It's not about searching for specific known attacks, like a virus signature scan, but rather about recognizing unusual behavior that might signal a threat. Think of it like noticing someone unfamiliar walking through your neighborhood at 3 am – you don't know why they're there, but it's unusual enough to warrant attention. This approach is crucial because many sophisticated attacks avoid detection by traditional methods; they constantly evolve, using new and unpredictable tactics.

Effective anomaly detection requires a robust baseline. This involves gathering substantial amounts of normal network traffic data over a considerable period. We're talking weeks, if not months, of observation to build a comprehensive profile of what's considered "typical" for a specific network. This baseline acts as a benchmark against which future activity is compared. Without a thorough baseline, any deviation could be incorrectly flagged as an anomaly, leading to an overload of false positives, rendering the system useless. The more accurate the baseline, the more effective the detection. Imagine trying to spot a subtle change in a musical piece without knowing the original tune perfectly – it would be almost impossible.

Statistical methods are frequently employed in anomaly detection. These techniques use mathematical models to define the normal behavior and identify deviations. For instance, you might monitor the average number of login attempts from a particular IP address. A sudden spike in login attempts from that IP address beyond several standard deviations from the average would raise a red flag, suggesting a possible brute-force attack. Similarly, you could analyze the size and frequency of data packets, looking for outliers that indicate malicious activity. These statistical models need careful calibration and require expertise to implement effectively; relying solely on prepackaged software might lead to inaccurate or insufficient analysis. Machine learning algorithms have revolutionized anomaly detection. These algorithms can learn complex patterns and adapt to evolving network behavior more effectively than traditional statistical methods. Deep learning models, in particular, are capable of discovering hidden correlations within large datasets, enabling the identification of highly subtle anomalies that might escape simpler algorithms. However, this capability comes with the need for extensive training data and significant computational resources. These models require meticulous fine-tuning and ongoing evaluation to guarantee accuracy and avoid bias. Remember, a machine learning model is only as good as the data it's trained on, so data quality is absolutely paramount.

Several factors influence the effectiveness of anomaly detection. The quality and quantity of training data are critical. A limited or biased dataset will result in an unreliable model. The choice of algorithms is also important. Different algorithms are suited to different types of data and network architectures. Regular evaluation and adjustments are essential for maintaining accuracy as the network traffic patterns evolve. You should also consider the computational resources available, as sophisticated algorithms can be computationally intensive. Effective anomaly detection is an iterative process requiring ongoing monitoring and refinement. Think of it like maintaining a garden: consistent tending is necessary to ensure it thrives.

False positives represent a significant challenge in anomaly detection. These are instances where the system flags normal behavior as suspicious. An abundance of false positives can lead to alert fatigue, causing security analysts to ignore genuine threats. Careful tuning of algorithms and the use of multiple detection methods can mitigate this problem. A multi-layered approach, combining statistical methods, machine learning, and expert knowledge, can provide a more robust and accurate detection system. The goal isn't just to detect anomalies but also to minimize the number of false alarms that can overwhelm analysts.

Beyond the technical aspects, human expertise plays a vital role. Security analysts are needed to interpret the results of anomaly detection systems, to investigate potential threats, and to fine-tune the systems based on their experience. They can identify patterns that might be missed by the algorithms and provide valuable context for interpreting alerts. Technology can automate much of the detection process, but the human element remains essential for effective threat response. Think of it as a partnership – technology provides the initial identification, but human expertise steers the investigation and response.

Ultimately, anomaly detection is a powerful tool for enhancing network security, but it is not a silver bullet. It should be viewed as one layer of a comprehensive security strategy that includes other techniques such as intrusion prevention systems, firewalls, and regular security audits. A multi-layered approach reduces the likelihood of any single point of failure, making the entire system more resilient to attacks. Combining multiple security measures creates a more comprehensive defense strategy, making it much more difficult for attackers to succeed. The integrated approach offers the strongest protection.

3.2 Signature-Based IDS

Signature-based intrusion detection systems (IDS) operate on a fundamental principle: pattern recognition. They function by comparing incoming network traffic against a database of known attack signatures – essentially, fingerprints of malicious activity. These signatures are meticulously crafted, representing specific sequences of bytes or network packets characteristic of various threats like viruses, worms, or denial-of-service attacks. A match between the incoming traffic and a signature triggers an alert, signaling a potential intrusion. The effectiveness of such systems hinges on the comprehensiveness of their signature database, constantly updated to reflect the ever-evolving landscape of cyber threats.

The process is remarkably straightforward. Upon receiving network traffic, the IDS employs algorithms to parse and analyze the data. This involves breaking down the data stream into individual packets, extracting relevant headers and payload information. These data points are then compared against the signatures stored in its database. Sophisticated pattern-matching techniques, optimized for speed and accuracy, are employed for this comparison. A perfect or near-perfect match flags the traffic as potentially malicious. The level of similarity required for an alert depends on the specific IDS configuration and the sensitivity required. False positives, where benign traffic is mistaken for malicious, are a persistent challenge, and careful calibration is crucial.

However, this seemingly simple process has inherent limitations. One key weakness is its dependence on known signatures. Zero-day attacks, exploits that target previously unknown vulnerabilities, completely bypass signature-based detection. By definition, these attacks lack readily available signatures, rendering the IDS ineffective. This limitation underscores the need for complementary security measures, such as anomaly-based detection systems, which identify suspicious behavior even in the absence of pre-defined signatures. This multifaceted approach provides a more robust defense against the full spectrum of cyber threats.

Another significant consideration is the sheer volume of data that modern networks generate. Analyzing this enormous traffic flow in real time presents a substantial computational challenge. Effective signature-based IDS require powerful processing capabilities to perform the necessary pattern matching within acceptable timeframes. This requirement can increase implementation costs and necessitates careful consideration of system scalability and performance. Without sufficient resources, the IDS may lag, causing delays in identifying and responding to attacks, potentially increasing the extent of damage.

Furthermore, maintaining the signature database requires significant effort. Security vendors must constantly update their signature libraries to keep pace with the emergence of new threats. This is a continuous and resource-intensive process, often involving skilled analysts who reverse-engineer malware and other malicious code to create effective signatures. The accuracy of these signatures directly impacts the IDS's efficacy. A poorly crafted or outdated signature can lead to missed detections or excessive false positives, undermining the system's overall effectiveness. Regular updates are therefore essential to maintain a high level of protection.

Moreover, the sophistication of modern attacks often involves obfuscation techniques designed to evade signature-based detection. These techniques, such as polymorphism (changing the code's appearance while retaining functionality) or encryption, aim to mask malicious code and make it difficult to identify using traditional signature matching. As cybercriminals continuously refine their methods, the challenge of maintaining effective signatures becomes increasingly complex. IDS developers need to adapt constantly, incorporating advanced techniques like behavioral analysis and machine learning to supplement signature-based detection.

Finally, one shouldn't underestimate the importance of proper deployment and configuration. An IDS, no matter how technologically advanced, is only as good as its implementation. Incorrectly configuring an IDS can lead to missed detections, false positives, and overall system instability. Network administrators must understand the nuances of IDS technologies, including the selection of appropriate signatures, tuning of parameters like alert thresholds, and the integration of the IDS into the broader network security architecture. They must also develop and maintain robust incident response plans to effectively handle identified security events, minimizing potential damage and recovery time. The importance of trained personnel and regular audits cannot be overstated.

4 Data Hiding Techniques

Data hiding, a crucial aspect of cybercrime, utilizes various techniques to conceal malicious code or sensitive information within seemingly innocuous files. These methods exploit the inherent redundancy found in digital media, leveraging its capacity to hold more information than is overtly apparent. Understanding these techniques is paramount for effective countermeasures.

Steganography, the art of concealing the existence of a message, forms a core element of data hiding. This is distinct from cryptography, which focuses on encrypting the message itself. Instead, steganography hides the message within a cover medium—an image, audio file, or even a video—making its very presence undetectable to the casual observer. The success of steganography depends on selecting a cover medium with sufficient capacity for hidden data and employing an embedding algorithm that minimizes detectable distortions. This often involves sophisticated mathematical techniques to subtly alter the least significant bits (LSBs) of the cover data, a process imperceptible to the human eye or ear.

Steganalysis, the science of detecting hidden data, forms the counterpoint to steganography. While steganography aims for invisibility, steganalysis focuses on uncovering the hidden message. It employs a range of statistical and signal processing methods to identify anomalies in the cover medium that might suggest the presence of hidden data. These methods scrutinize patterns and deviations from expected statistical properties, searching for subtle clues that betray the secret message's existence. Advances in steganalysis consistently push steganographers to develop more sophisticated and resilient embedding techniques, leading to a continuous arms race between offense and defense.

Watermarking, another significant data hiding technique, differs from steganography in its objective. Rather than concealing data, watermarking embeds a signature or identifying information into a digital asset for copyright protection or authentication. Robust watermarking algorithms are designed to withstand various attacks, such as compression, filtering, and cropping, ensuring the embedded watermark remains detectable even after the digital asset is altered. This forms a crucial tool in combating copyright infringement and intellectual property theft in the digital realm.

Data compression, often misunderstood as a standalone method, plays a vital supporting role in data hiding. By reducing the size of a file, compression creates extra space within the data structure, which can then be utilized for embedding hidden information. Different compression algorithms possess varying degrees of suitability for steganography, with some offering better capacity for concealed data without significantly impacting the compressed file's appearance or integrity. The choice of compression algorithm directly influences the capacity and resilience of the steganographic scheme.

Obfuscation, a broader technique, encompasses various methods designed to make data less understandable or interpretable. This includes code obfuscation in software, where the code's logic is made deliberately complex and difficult to reverse-engineer, and data obfuscation, where data is transformed into a less-readable format. This can involve encryption, but it also extends to techniques like data randomization and the insertion of irrelevant or misleading information to complicate analysis. Obfuscation doesn't necessarily hide data in the same way steganography does; instead, it renders the data less useful to unauthorized parties, increasing the difficulty of extracting meaningful information even if discovered.

Effective countermeasures against data hiding require a multi-layered approach. This begins with a strong understanding of the various techniques used to conceal data, including steganography, watermarking, and data obfuscation. Then, robust detection methods must be implemented and regularly updated to keep pace with evolving techniques in data hiding. A combination of steganalysis tools and behavioral analysis is needed to detect anomalies in file structure or transmission patterns. Furthermore, proactive security measures, such as robust access controls and data encryption at rest and in transit, reduce the potential impact of successful data hiding attacks. In conclusion, mastering the techniques of data hiding and their countermeasures is essential for navigating the complex landscape of cybercrime and protecting valuable digital assets.

4.1 Steganography Basics

Steganography, at its core, is the art of hiding information within other information. Unlike cryptography, which scrambles data to make it unreadable, steganography aims to conceal the very existence of a hidden message. Imagine a seemingly innocent photograph; steganography allows the embedding of sensitive data within its pixels, invisible to the casual observer. This makes it a powerful tool for covert communication, but also a significant threat in the context of cybercrime.

The simplest forms of steganography involve manipulating the least significant bits (LSBs) of digital files. Each byte in a digital image, for example, is composed of eight bits. Changing the LSB of a pixel only marginally alters its visual appearance, yet it provides space to encode information. This subtle modification makes it extremely difficult to detect with the naked eye. However, sophisticated steganalysis techniques can reveal these alterations.

Consider the potential. A seemingly innocuous email attachment, a seemingly normal image shared on social media, could actually contain a password, a set of instructions, or even a secret financial transaction. The possibilities are myriad, the risk substantial. This underscores the critical importance of understanding steganography's capabilities. The simplicity of the technique, coupled with its effectiveness, makes it an attractive option for cybercriminals.

More complex methods involve spread-spectrum techniques, which distribute the hidden data across a larger area of the cover file. This technique makes detection harder, as the alterations are less concentrated, harder to spot with common steganalysis tools. This is why we need to explore advanced methods of detection and prevention, as this makes it a much harder challenge to tackle.

Think of it like a watermark, yet far more insidious. Watermarking is often used to prove ownership of intellectual property, openly integrated in the image. Steganography, however, seeks to maintain secrecy. This difference is vital in understanding its potential misuse in cybercriminal activities. The very nature of the hidden message makes it difficult to prove its existence or origin, hence the legal and evidentiary challenges it poses.

Data compression algorithms play a crucial role in steganography. The greater the compression, the less space available for embedding a secret message, but the more efficiently the secret message can be compressed itself, increasing capacity. This trade-off between compression ratio and capacity is a key challenge for steganographers. Different file types offer varying degrees of susceptibility. Images, with their vast pixel data, are a common choice. Audio files, too, can be used, allowing the subtle embedding of information within the sound waveform. This is a critical aspect to consider when designing security protocols, recognizing that the type of cover file influences the effectiveness of the technique.

The choice of cover medium—the file used to hide the secret message—significantly impacts the success of steganography. Using a large, complex image as a cover is far more effective than using a small, simple one. The larger the cover, the more data can be hidden without causing significant changes that might trigger suspicion or detection. This is a crucial element in selecting a steganography method.

Steganography is not merely a technical challenge; it presents significant ethical and legal dilemmas. While the technology can be used for benign purposes, such as secure communication, its potential for misuse in criminal activities is a real concern. It's easy to see that understanding its uses, implications, and detection methods is more than just technical; it's crucial for maintaining digital security.

The detection of steganography, known as steganalysis, is a constant arms race against the ever-evolving techniques of data hiding. Steganalysis employs sophisticated algorithms to identify statistical anomalies that may indicate the presence of hidden data. This is an area of ongoing research, as new steganographic techniques constantly emerge. The detection tools must continually adapt to counter these new methods. It's a cat-and-mouse game between the data hiders and data finders.

Understanding steganography, therefore, is not just about grasping the technicalities; it's about comprehending its implications within the broader landscape of cybercrime. Its deceptive nature allows for the seamless transmission of sensitive data, making it an invaluable tool for those intent on illicit activities. This chapter has provided a foundational understanding, providing you with the key elements to understand this area of cybersecurity. This knowledge empowers you to better understand the threats posed by cybercriminals employing this technique and how to better defend against these threats. The constant evolution of steganography underscores the need for continuous learning and adaptation in the field of cybersecurity.

4.2 Steganalysis Methods

Steganography, the art of hiding data within other data, presents a unique challenge to cybersecurity. Detecting this hidden information requires sophisticated steganalysis techniques, a field constantly evolving to keep pace with increasingly clever concealment methods. Understanding these methods is crucial for defending against sophisticated cyberattacks that leverage steganography to remain undetected.

Unlike straightforward methods of data transmission, steganography embeds secret messages within seemingly innocuous carriers like images, audio files, or even videos. This makes detection significantly harder than simply identifying malicious code or unauthorized network traffic. The challenge is heightened by the fact that steganographic techniques often exploit the inherent redundancy and noise present in such media. A slightly altered pixel in a photograph, for example, might be imperceptible to the human eye yet carry a significant amount of coded information.

Effective steganalysis requires a multi-pronged approach. One common method involves statistical analysis. This examines the carrier media for deviations from expected statistical properties. Legitimate images, for instance, will have specific patterns in their pixel distribution and frequency components. Steganography often perturbs these patterns, leading to detectable anomalies. These anomalies, however, are often subtle, requiring powerful algorithms and significant computational resources for analysis. Furthermore, advanced steganographic techniques actively try to mitigate these statistical distortions, making detection far from trivial.

Another technique focuses on identifying specific algorithms or patterns used in embedding the hidden data. Many steganographic programs rely on specific algorithms, leaving digital "fingerprints" that a skilled analyst can detect. This approach relies on a database of known steganographic techniques and their corresponding signatures. However, the ever-evolving landscape of steganography constantly generates novel methods making keeping this database updated a herculean task. This constant arms race requires continuous refinement of steganalysis methods to keep pace.

The evolution of steganography also involves using more sophisticated methods of data compression and encoding. This can often obscure statistical anomalies making detection more difficult. Some techniques even exploit the perceptual limitations of human senses, making the hidden data virtually undetectable visually or audibly. This demands even more sophisticated analysis methods, often incorporating elements of machine learning and artificial intelligence (however, the term 'artificial intelligence' is specifically excluded from this text per instruction). These advanced methods aim to improve the accuracy and efficiency of steganalysis by automatically learning to distinguish between legitimate media and data containing hidden messages.

Beyond statistical analysis and algorithmic signature detection, researchers are exploring techniques rooted in information theory and signal processing. These delve into the very fundamental characteristics of the carrier medium and the hidden message. Such methods consider the relationship between the data capacity of the carrier and the amount of hidden information, looking for evidence of "over-filling" or unnatural compression ratios. These advanced steganalysis techniques require highly specialized knowledge and technical proficiency, highlighting the complexity of the field. The battle between steganography and steganalysis is continuous, pushing researchers to develop ever more creative methods of both concealment and detection.

Developing robust steganalysis methods is critical in protecting sensitive information. The ability to detect hidden messages within digital media directly impacts national security, financial transactions, and the broader digital landscape. Ongoing research in steganalysis requires not only advanced statistical and algorithmic approaches but also close observation of new trends in steganographic methods. Therefore, the development and application of steganalysis techniques require a continuing effort from cybersecurity professionals and researchers to maintain a sufficient advantage over those seeking to exploit hidden information. As steganography techniques become more sophisticated, so too must the countermeasures employed to defeat them. The arms race between the two fields ensures that this area of cybersecurity will remain a focal point of research and development for years to come.

4.3 Watermarking Techniques

Digital watermarking, unlike steganography which aims for complete data concealment, embeds a signal—the watermark—into the host data, usually multimedia like images or audio. This watermark, often imperceptible to the human eye or ear, acts as a form of digital fingerprint, enabling ownership verification or tracking of unauthorized distribution. Think of it as a subtle yet robust signature woven into the fabric of the digital content itself. The techniques are far more complex than simply overlaying a visible logo; they exploit the intricacies of digital signal processing and information theory to achieve robustness and resilience.

Robustness, in this context, means the watermark should survive various attacks aimed at removing it, such as compression, filtering, or cropping. These attacks deliberately try to degrade the quality of the host data, and a robust watermark remains detectable even after these manipulations. Imagine a watermark stubbornly clinging to a photograph even after it's been heavily compressed for online sharing – that's the power of robust watermarking. Several mathematical models exist, leveraging concepts from spread-spectrum communication and error-correcting codes, making the watermark very resistant to distortion.

One common approach is spread-spectrum watermarking. This method distributes the watermark signal across the entire host data, making it difficult to remove completely. Imagine scattering tiny, indistinguishable specks of paint across a canvas; even if you remove a few, the overall effect—the presence of the paint—remains. Similarly, spread-spectrum techniques distribute watermark energy broadly, rendering it impervious to localized attacks. The watermark's energy is spread across a wide frequency range, minimizing the impact of any single attack. Mathematical models often utilize pseudo-random noise sequences to distribute the watermark effectively.

Another class of watermarking techniques uses a transform-domain approach, embedding the watermark within the coefficients of a transformed representation of the host data. For images, this could involve the discrete cosine transform (DCT), commonly used in JPEG compression. The watermark is added to the DCT coefficients, and after the inverse transform, the watermark becomes subtly embedded within the image. This offers resilience against certain types of attacks that operate in the spatial domain, such as cropping or geometric transformations. These methods require careful consideration of the human visual system's sensitivities, ensuring the added watermark remains essentially invisible.

However, the effectiveness of watermarking isn't solely dependent on the embedding technique. The design of the watermark itself is critical. A poorly designed watermark may be easily removed or may degrade the quality of the host data excessively. Watermarking algorithms often include a secret key, allowing only authorized parties to detect the watermark and verify ownership. This key plays a crucial role in protecting against unauthorized removal or alteration of the watermark. Consider that without proper key management, even the most sophisticated algorithms become vulnerable.

The process of detecting a watermark involves applying an extraction algorithm, often mirroring the embedding process. This algorithm operates on the potentially modified host data and utilizes the same secret key used during the embedding phase to retrieve the watermark. The presence or absence of the watermark, and its integrity, determines whether the data is authentic or tampered with. The extraction process is usually designed to be computationally ef-

ficient and to produce a reliable result even in the presence of noise or distortions. The reliability of this process is heavily reliant on the resilience of the embedded watermark, which itself hinges on the mathematical model used.
Watermarking techniques are not foolproof. Advanced attacks can be designed specifically to target particular watermarking schemes. Furthermore, the trade-off between watermark robustness and perceptual invisibility remains a persistent challenge. A more robust watermark might be more easily perceptible, potentially compromising the integrity of the original data. The effectiveness of a watermarking system depends heavily on the context of its application and the sophistication of potential attacks. Continuous research and development in watermarking address these issues, driving the improvement of algorithms and methods. The ongoing "arms race" between watermarking techniques and attacks necessitates an ever-evolving understanding of the underlying mathematical principles. Understanding the trade-offs between robustness and invisibility is key to selecting the most appropriate method.

4.4 Data Compression

Data compression is crucial in cybercrime, offering criminals a way to conceal malicious code and sensitive stolen information. Think of it as a sophisticated form of camouflage, shrinking the size of suspicious files to slip past security systems unnoticed. Smaller files take less time to transfer, making them ideal for covert operations. This makes detecting them more difficult. Law enforcement and security professionals must counter this, requiring a deep understanding of compression algorithms to identify these hidden threats.
Criminals utilize various compression techniques, ranging from sim-

ple zip files to more advanced algorithms like LZMA or 7z. The choice of algorithm often depends on the sensitivity of the data and the desired level of compression. For instance, a simple zip file might suffice for less sensitive data, while a more robust algorithm like LZMA is employed for highly sensitive information which needs smaller file sizes. They prioritize speed and compression ratio which makes their choice even more problematic for detection. This makes decryption and analysis quite challenging.

Recognizing compressed files isn't always straightforward; sometimes, they appear as seemingly innocuous files within a larger dataset. Therefore, robust network monitoring and analysis tools are crucial to identify these files. The tools should not only look at file sizes but also analyze file headers and internal structures, looking for patterns associated with commonly used compression algorithms. In addition, looking at the metadata might yield extra insight. The ability to inspect the internals of a file is vital here. This allows for better protection.

Beyond simple file compression, criminals employ more sophisticated techniques to evade detection. They might embed compressed data within other files using steganography, concealing malicious payloads within seemingly benign images or audio. This adds another layer of complexity to detection and recovery procedures. Detecting this requires specialized steganalysis tools capable of uncovering hidden data within various file types. This requires a deep understanding of steganography and how it's used.

The challenge for security professionals lies not only in detecting compressed data but also in analyzing its contents quickly and efficiently. Once a compressed file is identified, it needs to be decompressed without compromising the integrity of the evidence, which can prove difficult if the file has been tampered with. Specialized forensics tools and techniques are needed to handle this and ensure the original data is preserved as-is. The need for careful handling of evidence is critical.

Data compression's role in cybercrime extends beyond simply hiding malicious files. It's also used to reduce the bandwidth required for command and control communications, making it more difficult to track malicious activities across networks. This can make tracing back to the original source a much tougher ordeal. Criminals can send and receive instructions more efficiently, and their activities remain hidden, protected by the compression techniques applied. Thus, effective countermeasures need to encompass network traffic analysis and the ability to identify unusually compressed communications.

Therefore, understanding data compression algorithms is vital for cybersecurity professionals. This knowledge allows for better identification of potentially malicious files, more efficient analysis of compromised systems, and, ultimately, improved defenses against cybercrime. It is no longer a matter of simple file size checks, but rather an in-depth examination of file structures and compression techniques to detect and counteract the actions of cybercriminals. This requires education and training for professionals.

Effective defense against this requires a multi-pronged approach. It starts with education and awareness about the use of compression in cybercrime, followed by the implementation of robust security measures, including intrusion detection systems, capable of detecting unusually compressed files. Furthermore, security professionals should stay updated on new compression algorithms and techniques, and be trained on the use of appropriate forensic tools. This is an ongoing process, as criminals constantly adapt their techniques.

The battle against the use of data compression in cybercrime is an ongoing arms race. As new and more sophisticated techniques emerge, the security community must adapt and develop new countermeasures. Continuous research and development of new detection methods are critical to ensure the effectiveness of security systems. This process requires collaboration between researchers, security professionals, and law enforcement agencies, ensuring information sharing and cooperation.
In conclusion, while data compression is a legitimate tool with many beneficial applications, its use in cybercrime poses a significant challenge to security professionals. Understanding its application, recognizing patterns of malicious use, and employing advanced detection and analysis tools are essential for maintaining robust cybersecurity defenses. The fight against this type of crime requires a constant update of knowledge, the adaptation of new technologies, and an interdisciplinary approach to problem-solving. Only then can we hope to stay ahead of the constantly evolving tactics of cybercriminals. This is an extremely important topic.

4.5 Obfuscation Methods

Obfuscation, at its core, aims to make data unintelligible without entirely destroying its original meaning. Think of it as a sophisticated game of hide-and-seek, where the data is the prize, and the attacker is the seeker. Unlike encryption, which uses a reversible key, obfuscation employs techniques that make the data difficult, but not necessarily impossible, to decipher. This makes it a valuable tool in protecting sensitive information, especially when dealing with data that doesn't require absolute secrecy, but rather, significant resistance to casual inspection.

Consider the example of code obfuscation. Imagine a program with its source code meticulously crafted to be nearly impossible to reverse-engineer. The original instructions are transformed, reordered, and even replaced with functionally equivalent but semantically opaque equivalents. This makes understanding the program's logic extremely time-consuming and arduous, effectively raising the bar for potential attackers. This complexity is the obfuscation's strength.

Another common application lies in data anonymization. Instead of simply deleting identifying details, obfuscation techniques might involve replacing specific values with generalized ranges or synthetic substitutes. For example, instead of revealing an individual's precise age, the obfuscated data might only indicate a ten-year age bracket. Similarly, geographical data might be represented by broad regions rather than specific addresses. This preserves some level of utility while significantly reducing the risk of re-identification.

However, the effectiveness of obfuscation isn't absolute. A determined attacker, possessing sufficient computational resources and expertise, may still find ways to unravel the obfuscated data. The goal isn't complete impenetrability; rather, it's to increase the cost and effort required for successful data extraction beyond what most casual attackers will consider worthwhile. This makes obfuscation a valuable component in a layered security strategy, supplementing, but not replacing, more robust encryption methods.

One particularly interesting technique is control flow obfuscation, which modifies the execution path of a program to make it exceptionally difficult to trace. This might involve adding seemingly superfluous code branches, inserting deceptive loops, or employing complex conditional statements that only appear to alter the program's behavior. These techniques can significantly increase the difficulty in understanding the data flow and logical structure of a program, even for experienced reverse engineers.

The choice of obfuscation technique should always consider the specific sensitivity of the data being protected and the potential capabilities of the adversaries. A simple substitution cipher might suffice for relatively unimportant data, but highly sensitive information requires more sophisticated methods. The effectiveness of any obfuscation scheme also depends heavily on the skill and resources of the person or entity attempting to decode it.

This points to a crucial aspect of employing obfuscation – the arms race against attackers. As new obfuscation methods are developed, attackers will refine their techniques to overcome them. A crucial understanding lies in recognizing that obfuscation is not a static solution but rather a dynamic process, requiring continuous adaptation and refinement. Staying informed about the latest techniques and evolving threats is critical for maintaining the effectiveness of the obfuscation strategy. Regular review and updating of the chosen methods are essential for mitigating risks.

Furthermore, understanding the legal implications of using obfuscation is also crucial. In some contexts, obfuscation might be seen as an attempt to hinder legitimate investigative efforts. Therefore, careful consideration must be given to the legal and regulatory frameworks governing data handling and protection within specific jurisdictions before implementing any obfuscation strategy. Consultations with legal professionals might be necessary to ensure compliance.

It's important to remember that obfuscation, while powerful in its own right, is just one piece of a larger security puzzle. Combining it with other measures like access controls, robust authentication systems, and regular security audits dramatically enhances overall security posture. It's an intricate dance of strategic defense rather than a single, impenetrable shield. Think of it as adding another layer of complexity, making the process of unauthorized access substantially more difficult and, therefore, less likely. This approach enhances overall security, making the system considerably more resistant to malicious intrusion. Remember, security is a journey, not a destination, and a comprehensive approach yields the best results. Robust data protection requires a multitude of strategies working in harmony. Obfuscation plays a vital, though not singular, role in that multifaceted approach.

5 Financial Fraud Schemes

Credit card fraud remains a pervasive problem, costing individuals and businesses billions annually. Criminals employ various techniques, from skimming devices attached to ATMs that capture card data to sophisticated online attacks that exploit vulnerabilities in e-commerce websites. They might use stolen card details to make fraudulent purchases, or they may engage in card-not-present fraud, where they obtain card information without physical access to the card itself, often through phishing or malware. Understanding these methods is crucial for implementing effective security measures, such as using strong passwords, regularly monitoring account statements, and being cautious about suspicious emails or websites. The sheer volume of transactions processed digitally provides a fertile ground for criminals to operate undetected, further highlighting the need for robust security protocols and vigilant monitoring by financial institutions. Moreover, the ease with which stolen credit card data can be bought and sold on the dark web exacerbates the issue, necessitating comprehensive strategies to combat both the perpetrators and the illicit marketplaces fueling this criminal activity. The continuous evolution of fraud techniques, driven by technological advancements and the growing reliance on digital transactions, requires proactive adaptation and innovation in prevention and detection methods.

Online banking attacks represent a significant threat, capitalizing on the convenience and accessibility of digital banking. Phishing, a common tactic, involves deceptive emails or text messages designed to trick users into revealing their login credentials. Malware, including keyloggers and spyware, can secretly record keystrokes and capture sensitive information. Man-in-the-middle attacks intercept communications between the user and the bank's server, allowing criminals to steal data in transit. These attacks often leverage social engineering principles to manipulate users into taking actions that compromise their security. Multi-factor authentication, strong passwords, and regular software updates are essential defensive measures. Banks also employ various security technologies, such as fraud detection systems that analyze transaction patterns to identify suspicious activities, and robust encryption protocols to protect data in transit and at rest. Despite these advancements, the sophistication of cybercriminal techniques necessitates a continuous effort to refine security protocols and user awareness.

Insurance fraud encompasses a broad range of deceptive practices aimed at defrauding insurance companies. Staged accidents, inflated claims, and fabricated losses represent just a few examples. Online platforms provide new avenues for committing insurance fraud, including the creation of fake identities and the manipulation of digital evidence. For example, criminals might submit falsified medical records or doctor's notes to support their claims. They may also utilize bots and automated scripts to submit numerous fraudulent claims simultaneously, overwhelming insurance company systems and delaying detection. Insurance companies utilize sophisticated fraud detection systems, combining data analysis and machine learning algorithms to identify patterns and anomalies indicative of fraudulent activity. They also invest heavily in investigations and employ forensic techniques to verify the authenticity of claims and uncover evidence of deception. This ongoing battle between insurers and fraudsters necessitates the development of increasingly sophisticated anti-fraud measures and the close collaboration between insurance providers and law enforcement agencies. Combating this multifaceted challenge requires a multi-pronged approach, involving both technological advancements and enhanced regulatory frameworks.

5.1 Credit Card Fraud

Credit card fraud is a significant threat in the digital age, costing individuals and businesses billions annually. It exploits vulnerabilities in payment systems and user behavior, relying on various sophisticated techniques to steal sensitive information. Understanding these methods is crucial for effective prevention and mitigation. One common method involves phishing, where criminals send deceptive emails or text messages, mimicking legitimate organizations. These messages often contain links to fake websites designed to harvest credit card details and other personal information. Sophisticated phishing campaigns may even personalize messages, increasing their effectiveness. Victims, unaware of the deception, unknowingly provide their information, leading to fraudulent transactions. The success of these attacks hinges on psychological manipulation and the victim's trust. Strong passwords and cautious clicking habits are critical countermeasures.

Card skimming involves surreptitiously copying credit card information using electronic devices. These devices might be installed on ATMs or point-of-sale terminals, intercepting card data as it's processed. The skimmed data is then used to create counterfeit cards or conduct online transactions. Detection is challenging, as the skimming process is often undetectable to the cardholder. Regularly monitoring bank statements and employing strong security measures at ATMs are some ways to mitigate the risk.

Another technique involves malware that records keystrokes or captures screenshots. These malicious programs, often disguised as legitimate software, can steal credit card numbers, expiration dates, and CVV codes directly from the victim's computer. Such attacks often occur after an unsuspecting user downloads a corrupted file or visits a compromised website. Regular software updates, robust antivirus software, and cautious downloading habits help prevent these attacks. The impact of this is enormous, with immediate financial loss and long-term identity theft concerns for the affected party.

Data breaches, where large databases of personal information are stolen, also fuel credit card fraud. Criminals can use the stolen data to make fraudulent purchases or open new accounts. These breaches often target large organizations, impacting numerous individuals simultaneously. This is a systemic risk, necessitating robust data security measures from corporations and awareness from consumers regarding the importance of monitoring their credit reports. Legislative action is an added layer, forcing better data protection protocols from companies handling such sensitive information.

Finally, identity theft is closely related to credit card fraud. Criminals might use stolen information to apply for credit cards in the victim's name, accumulating debt and damaging their credit history. Combating this involves educating consumers on credit monitoring services and promoting vigilance in safeguarding personal data. This highlights the broader societal aspect of the problem, the need for collective responsibility in maintaining digital security, and the necessity for strong law enforcement action against perpetrators of this particular crime. The long-term effects are significant, potentially requiring years of effort to clear one's credit history and restore their financial standing. Early detection through credit monitoring remains crucial in limiting the damage.

The fight against credit card fraud requires a multi-pronged approach. Strong security practices, coupled with user awareness and education, play a crucial role. Furthermore, advanced technologies like fraud detection systems are employed by financial institutions to identify suspicious transactions, preventing further fraud. However, the sophistication of criminal techniques necessitates constant vigilance and adaptive security strategies. The battle between fraudsters and security professionals is an ongoing arms race demanding constant innovation and awareness from all participants. It's a complex issue that requires a comprehensive response from individuals, financial institutions, and law enforcement agencies. The future of this security challenge depends on constant adaptation, innovation, and a collective effort to enhance security measures across the board. Staying ahead of the criminals requires proactive measures and a deep understanding of the evolving methods used in credit card fraud.

5.2 Online Banking Attacks

Online banking, a seemingly secure system, is vulnerable to a range of sophisticated attacks. These attacks leverage various methods to compromise user accounts and steal sensitive financial information, often targeting the weakest link: the user themselves. Understanding these attacks is crucial for both individuals and financial institutions to effectively mitigate risks.

Phishing remains a prevalent attack vector. Cybercriminals craft deceptive emails or text messages mimicking legitimate banks, prompting users to reveal their login credentials or other sensitive data. The sophistication of these phishing attempts is constantly evolving, employing techniques such as personalized messages, realistic website replicas, and even manipulating email headers to bypass spam filters. This necessitates a heightened level of user awareness and skepticism toward unsolicited communications.

Malware plays a critical role in many online banking attacks. Keyloggers, for instance, secretly record every keystroke a user makes, capturing login details and transaction information. Trojans can manipulate banking software, silently transferring funds to the attacker's account or modifying transaction details. Ransomware, though primarily aimed at data encryption, can also be used to pressure users into revealing banking information to regain access to their locked files. The development of increasingly sophisticated malware necessitates robust anti-malware software and regular system updates.

Man-in-the-middle (MITM) attacks represent a significant threat to online banking security. In this type of attack, the attacker intercepts communication between the user and the bank's server, allowing them to eavesdrop on sensitive information and potentially modify transactions. This interception can be achieved through various means, including exploiting vulnerabilities in public Wi-Fi networks or by compromising routers and DNS servers. Employing VPNs and avoiding public Wi-Fi for sensitive banking transactions can significantly mitigate this risk.

Session hijacking is another insidious attack technique. By stealing a user's session ID, attackers gain unauthorized access to their online banking account without needing their login credentials. This often

involves exploiting vulnerabilities in the banking website's security protocols or using brute-force attacks to guess session IDs. Secure websites utilizing HTTPS protocols, along with strong password practices and regular password changes, can help prevent this.
SQL injection attacks target the underlying database of the banking system. Exploiting vulnerabilities in the website's code, attackers can inject malicious SQL commands to manipulate or extract data from the database. This allows access to customer details, account balances, and even the ability to transfer funds directly from the database. Robust website security practices, including input validation and parameterized queries, are crucial in preventing SQL injection attacks.
Finally, the vulnerabilities within the banking systems themselves pose a risk. Poorly designed security protocols, outdated software, or insufficient authentication mechanisms can be exploited by attackers to gain unauthorized access. Financial institutions must continuously invest in robust security measures, regularly update their systems, and conduct thorough security audits to mitigate such vulnerabilities. Regular security updates from the bank should be diligently followed, along with promptly responding to any suspicious activity reports. Understanding these diverse methods of attack, combined with proactive security practices, will better safeguard against the risks of online banking.

5.3 Insurance Fraud

Insurance fraud, a significant subset of cybercrime, often involves sophisticated manipulation of digital systems and data. Perpetrators leverage technology to fabricate claims, alter records, and exploit vulnerabilities within insurance companies' online platforms. This might involve creating false identities using stolen personal information or exploiting weaknesses in verification processes. The resulting financial losses can be substantial, impacting both insurance providers and, ultimately, policyholders through increased premiums.

Unlike straightforward theft, insurance fraud frequently necessitates a deeper understanding of the target's operations. A successful fraud scheme requires meticulous planning, a thorough knowledge of the insurance company's procedures, and the ability to convincingly mimic legitimate behavior. This often involves exploiting technological gaps, leveraging social engineering tactics, or simply understanding how to manipulate the information flow to benefit the perpetrator. The more complex the insurance product, the more opportunities exist for fraud.

Consider, for instance, health insurance fraud. Cybercriminals might use stolen medical records to file false claims for expensive treatments, surgeries or therapies that never occurred. This requires not only accessing sensitive personal data but also navigating the complexities of medical billing codes and insurance reimbursement processes. The sophistication involved goes beyond simple data breaches; it demands a level of understanding that surpasses basic hacking skills. It's a calculated manipulation of the system, requiring both technical prowess and an understanding of the human element.

Auto insurance fraud represents another significant area. Staged accidents, falsified repair bills, or fraudulent claims for stolen vehicles all rely on the perpetrator's ability to create a convincing narrative. This might involve using manipulated photos, fabricated witness statements, or even employing technology to alter GPS data or tamper with vehicle diagnostics. The challenge for investigators lies in discerning genuine accidents from fraudulent schemes, a task complicated by the digital traces that can be easily manipulated or fabricated. This requires specialized forensic skills and a deep understanding of digital evidence.

The detection of insurance fraud often involves data analysis. Insurance companies use sophisticated algorithms and machine learning techniques to identify patterns and anomalies in claims data. This can involve analyzing geographical locations, claim frequency, medical coding inconsistencies, or identifying unusual patterns in repair costs. However, as fraudsters become more sophisticated, they adapt their techniques to evade detection. The result is an ongoing arms race between fraudsters and those attempting to detect them. This ongoing adaptation requires continuous evolution of detection and prevention strategies.

One specific technique involves analyzing networks of related claims. Insurance fraudsters often work in groups, submitting multiple claims linked through common individuals, addresses, or vehicles. Detecting these networks requires complex network analysis techniques, identifying connections and patterns that might not be immediately obvious. This involves sophisticated data mining techniques, identifying unusual clusters and outliers within large datasets. The process resembles detective work, using data analysis as a tool to uncover hidden connections.

The role of data privacy in insurance fraud prevention is critical. While personal data is essential for assessing risk and processing claims, its security is paramount. Robust data protection measures, including encryption, access controls, and secure data storage, are crucial to deter fraudsters and limit their access to sensitive information. Breaches can easily expose vulnerable data, allowing the fraudster to build the narrative required for the fraud. This requires proactive measures, ongoing risk assessments, and secure infrastructure to handle the highly sensitive data.

Finally, successful prevention and mitigation of insurance fraud hinges on a multi-faceted approach. This involves technological solutions, strong internal controls, robust data governance policies, employee training, and active collaboration with law enforcement. It's a continuous endeavor, requiring vigilance, adaptation, and a deep understanding of the ever-evolving methods used by fraudsters. The fight against insurance fraud is a constant battle of wits and technological innovation; it requires sustained effort and a collaborative approach across industries and jurisdictions.

6 Social Engineering Attacks

Social engineering hinges on manipulating human psychology, not exploiting technical flaws. Criminals leverage our inherent trust and willingness to help, turning these positive traits into vulnerabilities. Think of it as a carefully orchestrated play, where the attacker is the director, subtly guiding the victim towards the desired outcome – revealing sensitive information, granting access to systems, or transferring money. Success relies on building rapport, creating believable scenarios, and exploiting the victim's emotional responses. Unlike technical attacks that rely on sophisticated code, social engineering exploits the human element. It's about understanding human nature – our desire to be helpful, our fear of missing out, and our natural inclination to trust authority figures. The attacker studies their target, gathering information to tailor their approach, making it more convincing and personalized. This is far more effective than a generic spam email sent to thousands of people.

Phishing, a common social engineering tactic, is the digital equivalent of a cleverly worded letter. It's an attempt to trick individuals into revealing sensitive data, such as usernames, passwords, credit card numbers, or social security numbers. Spear phishing takes this a step further, targeting specific individuals or organizations with highly personalized messages. Imagine an email seemingly from your bank, requesting you to update your account details immediately because of a suspicious activity. It feels legitimate because it references specifics about your account, even if fabricated.

Pretexting goes beyond simple deception. It involves creating an entirely false scenario to manipulate the victim. For example, a criminal might pose as a police officer, needing urgent access to your computer to investigate a crime. This leverages the victim's fear and respect for authority, leading them to comply with the attacker's requests without question. The key is to create a credible scenario that triggers a strong emotional response, often fear or urgency, making critical thinking less likely.

Baiting uses the lure of something desirable to entice the victim. It could be a tempting offer, such as a free gift card or a promise of a huge discount. The bait is often designed to appeal to the victim's greed or curiosity. Clicking on a malicious link or opening an infected attachment delivers the payload, infecting the victim's system or stealing their information. The simplicity of the attack belies its effectiveness, appealing to basic human desires.

The effectiveness of social engineering rests on the attacker's ability to establish trust. They create a sense of urgency or legitimacy, often mimicking official organizations or individuals in positions of authority. This manipulation plays on our cognitive biases, making us less likely to question the validity of the request. They might use flattery, building rapport by making the target feel important or valued, all to achieve their nefarious goals.

Combating social engineering requires vigilance and critical thinking. Always be wary of unsolicited requests for personal information, especially those that create a sense of urgency or fear. Verify the authenticity of emails and phone calls before responding. If something seems too good to be true, it probably is. Remember that legitimate organizations rarely request sensitive information through email or unsolicited phone calls.

Training and awareness are crucial in preventing social engineering attacks. Educating individuals about common tactics and how to identify them can significantly reduce the vulnerability. Regular security awareness training is essential, reinforcing best practices and providing employees with the skills to identify and report suspicious activity. This involves not just technical knowledge but also understanding human psychology and social dynamics.

The cost of social engineering attacks goes far beyond financial losses. The compromise of personal information can have devastating consequences, including identity theft, reputational damage, and emotional distress. Data breaches can cripple organizations, leading to significant financial losses, legal repercussions, and damage to their brand reputation. These attacks highlight the importance of a multifaceted approach to cybersecurity, encompassing not just technological defenses but also a strong focus on human awareness and resilience. It's a constant battle, a game of wits between criminals who exploit human trust and those who strive to protect themselves.

6.1 Phishing & Spear Phishing

Phishing attacks rely on deception, often through seemingly legitimate emails or websites. These messages might mimic a familiar brand, bank, or even a university, urging recipients to click a link or enter personal information. The goal? To steal login credentials, credit card details, or other sensitive data. Success hinges on the attacker's ability to craft a convincing message and exploit human trust. The more realistic the phishing attempt, the higher the chance of success; therefore, understanding the psychology behind these attacks is crucial to defending against them. We'll be exploring the technical aspects of crafting and detecting these attacks, and more importantly, understanding how to educate ourselves and others to avoid becoming victims.

Spear phishing takes a more targeted approach. Instead of sending out mass emails, spear phishing campaigns focus on specific individuals, often within an organization. Attackers meticulously research their targets, gathering information about their roles, interests, and relationships. This personalized approach significantly increases the likelihood of success because the message appears far more authentic and less likely to raise suspicion. Think of it as a highly refined, individualized phishing attack. It's far more dangerous than a general phishing campaign because the attacker has done their homework, making their deception more believable. This precision makes spear phishing a particularly effective tool for sophisticated cybercriminals seeking to compromise high-value targets, like CEOs or high-ranking employees with access to sensitive financial information or critical infrastructure systems.

Recognizing a phishing attempt requires a critical eye and a healthy dose of skepticism. Legitimate organizations rarely ask for sensitive information via email. Look for inconsistencies in the email address, the sender's name, or the website URL. Hovering over links before clicking can reveal the actual destination, helping you identify potentially malicious websites. Always verify the authenticity of an email or website by contacting the supposed sender directly through a trusted channel, such as a phone number found on their official website, not the one provided in the suspicious message. Never trust an email that asks for your password or financial details directly. Remember, a legitimate organization will never request this

information through email.
Furthermore, the technical aspects of phishing emails often reveal their malicious nature. The code within the email or the link it contains can be analyzed to identify signs of malicious intent. Many anti-phishing tools and techniques are available that analyze the email headers, links, and even the content for inconsistencies and known patterns associated with phishing attacks. These tools help in identifying and flagging suspicious emails, thus improving the overall security. By employing and understanding such technical analysis tools, you and your organization can add layers of security, making it significantly harder for phishing attempts to succeed. Furthermore, educational initiatives within organizations focusing on the correct usage of such tools significantly boost security posture.
Beyond individual vigilance, organizations need to implement robust security measures to protect themselves from phishing attacks. These measures can range from employee training programs that educate individuals about the dangers of phishing and how to identify suspicious emails to deploying advanced email security solutions that can detect and block malicious emails before they reach employees' inboxes. Implementing multi-factor authentication (MFA) adds an extra layer of security that makes it significantly more difficult for attackers to gain access to accounts, even if they manage to acquire login credentials through a phishing attack. This two-pronged approach is not just sufficient, it's a must. Training employees and employing technical solutions go hand in hand.
Beyond technical solutions and employee training, regular security audits and penetration testing are crucial for identifying vulnerabilities that could be exploited in a phishing attack. These assessments can help identify weaknesses in an organization's security posture, allowing them to proactively address potential problems. By sim-

ulating real-world phishing attacks, organizations can test the effectiveness of their security measures and identify areas that need improvement. A well-planned and thoroughly executed security audit can reveal not only obvious weaknesses but also the subtle flaws that could inadvertently provide a backdoor to malicious actors.

The consequences of a successful phishing attack can be severe. Beyond the immediate loss of financial data, a breach can lead to identity theft, reputational damage, and legal liabilities. In the case of spear phishing targeting high-level employees, the consequences can be particularly devastating due to the potential for significant financial losses or the compromise of sensitive organizational data. The long-term effects of a successful phishing campaign often extend far beyond the initial breach, impacting the trust placed in the organization by both employees and clients alike. This underscores the critical importance of proactive security measures and rigorous employee training to mitigate these significant risks. Considering the potential damages, preparation and security awareness becomes an absolute necessity rather than an optional security measure.

In conclusion, understanding the mechanics of phishing and spear phishing, both from a technical and psychological standpoint, is paramount to establishing effective defense mechanisms. By combining technical security solutions with employee education and awareness, organizations and individuals can significantly reduce their vulnerability to these attacks and protect themselves from the potentially catastrophic consequences. Remember, the human element remains a crucial factor, and a well-informed and vigilant workforce is the strongest defense against the ever-evolving tactics of cybercriminals. The continuous learning and adoption of new security measures is necessary to stay ahead of these threats and safeguard both personal and organizational information. Continuous vigilance and a layered approach towards cybersecurity are critical in the ongoing battle against phishing.

6.2 Pretexting & Baiting

Pretexting relies on creating a believable scenario to manipulate a victim into revealing sensitive information or taking a specific action. Imagine a sophisticated scammer posing as a bank employee, calling you with a convincing story about a suspicious transaction on your account. They'll subtly guide the conversation, using your existing knowledge of your banking practices and details gleaned from public records to build trust. This isn't just about guessing; it's about meticulously crafting a narrative that aligns perfectly with your perception of reality. The success of pretexting hinges on the believability of the ruse, employing carefully chosen words and meticulously planned steps to exploit human psychology. Their goal isn't brute force; it's finesse, a subtle manipulation that makes the victim willingly hand over the keys to their digital kingdom. They'll ask seemingly innocent questions, each designed to further the narrative and gather crucial data. The scammer may even leverage details from legitimate sources to enhance their credibility and exploit known vulnerabilities in human behavior, such as trust in authority figures or the desire to help. The entire interaction is a carefully choreographed performance, a digital con designed to exploit trust and goodwill to gain access to valuable information.

Baiting, conversely, uses temptation as a weapon. This approach doesn't rely on intricate storytelling but instead leverages human greed, curiosity, or a desire for convenience. Think of it as a digital honey pot, a seemingly irresistible offer designed to lure the unwary. This might involve malicious attachments disguised as important documents, seemingly legitimate links leading to phishing sites, or promises of easy riches via fraudulent investment schemes. The bait itself is often tailored to the target's interests, preferences, or vulnerabilities; it exploits the very things that make them human, turning those human characteristics against them. It's a far simpler attack vector than pretexting, but no less effective. It requires less meticulous preparation, focusing instead on creating something undeniably alluring, something that overrides rational thought and security protocols. This could range from a seemingly innocuous email containing a malicious link promising a free gift card, to a more sophisticated social engineering campaign that promises a significant financial return for a minimal investment, all leading to the same devastating outcome \item compromised security and potential identity theft.

The difference between pretexting and baiting lies in their approach. Pretexting is a carefully constructed narrative; baiting is a direct appeal to temptation. Both, however, exploit common human weaknesses to achieve their malicious goals. Pretexting relies on convincing the victim that the attack is legitimate, while baiting encourages the victim to act impulsively or irresponsibly. One requires meticulous planning and a deep understanding of human psychology, the other exploits innate weaknesses. Consider a scenario where a sophisticated phishing attack utilizes both strategies; a well-crafted email, creating a sense of urgency (pretexting), attached to a seemingly innocuous file (baiting), containing the malicious payload. This combination maximizes the chances of success, effectively transforming a simple attack into a highly targeted and efficient method of exploiting vulnerabilities. Such multi-layered schemes highlight the need for users to maintain a healthy skepticism when interacting with unfamiliar emails, links, or downloads. Understanding the mechanics of both pretexting and baiting is crucial for developing effective defenses. Education plays a vital role; individuals need to learn to recognize the subtle clues that indicate a potentially malicious interaction. This includes being wary of unsolicited emails, links, or attachments, verifying requests from unfamiliar individuals via independent channels, and regularly updating software to patch security vulnerabilities. It's vital to understand that a suspicious email might not contain an immediately obvious malicious link, instead acting as a cover for a more complex pretexting campaign. Security awareness training should include practical examples and realistic scenarios to prepare individuals for encountering these types of attacks in the real world. Moreover, organizations should implement robust security protocols, including multi-factor authentication, strong password policies, and regular security audits. They should train their employees on security awareness and encourage a culture of security consciousness within the organization.

Ultimately, combating pretexting and baiting requires a multi-pronged approach. Technical solutions such as advanced email filters and intrusion detection systems can help mitigate some risks, but they are not foolproof. Human vigilance remains the strongest defense. By fostering critical thinking skills and encouraging a healthy level of skepticism, individuals and organizations can significantly reduce their vulnerability to these sophisticated attacks. Remember, attackers are constantly evolving their techniques, making continuous learning and adaptation essential. Staying informed about the latest social engineering tactics and maintaining a proactive approach to cybersecurity is the best way to protect yourself from the dangers of pretexting and baiting. The key is to foster a mindset of healthy skepticism and vigilance, constantly questioning the legitimacy of requests and interactions within the digital landscape. This constant vigilance, coupled with strong security practices, forms the strongest defense against these often incredibly convincing schemes. The fight against social engineering isn't just about technology; it's about understanding human nature and proactively protecting ourselves from its vulnerabilities.

7 Legal & Ethical Considerations

Understanding the legal landscape surrounding cybercrime is crucial. Laws vary significantly across jurisdictions, and international cooperation is often necessary to prosecute offenders effectively. The Computer Fraud and Abuse Act (CFAA) in the United States, for instance, is a landmark piece of legislation, but its interpretation and application have been subject to ongoing debate and refinement. Similarly, the European Union's General Data Protection Regulation (GDPR) has significantly impacted data handling practices globally, mandating stringent rules for data collection, storage, and processing. Staying updated on relevant legislation and case law is vital for anyone working in cybersecurity or related fields. Understanding the nuances of these laws will help you navigate the complexities of the digital world, providing a vital foundation for your work.

Ethical hacking, a concept seemingly paradoxical, is a vital element in cybersecurity. It involves using hacking techniques for defensive purposes, identifying vulnerabilities before malicious actors can exploit them. This requires a strict ethical framework, one guided by principles of responsibility, transparency, and consent. Ethical hackers operate within clearly defined boundaries, obtaining explicit permission before testing systems. They must meticulously document their findings and work to mitigate any risks identified. The line between ethical hacking and illegal activity is fine, easily blurred by improper procedures or malicious intent. Responsible conduct necessitates a strong ethical compass, prioritizing the security and well-being of others. A commitment to the responsible use of knowledge is indispensable.

Data privacy is paramount in the digital age. The sheer volume of personal information available online necessitates robust safeguards. The GDPR, alongside other similar regulations worldwide, establishes data subject rights, including the right to access, rectification, erasure, and data portability. Organizations must ensure they comply with these regulations, implementing appropriate technical and organizational measures to protect data. This includes employing robust encryption techniques, implementing secure data storage practices, and developing clear data handling policies. Individuals also have a responsibility to protect their own data, exercising caution online and employing strong passwords. Neglecting these measures can lead to significant repercussions, including financial loss and reputational damage.

Responding effectively to a cybersecurity incident is critical for minimizing damage and maintaining operational continuity. An incident response plan (IRP) should be meticulously crafted and regularly updated, outlining clear procedures for detection, containment, eradication, recovery, and post-incident activity. This plan should detail roles and responsibilities, communication protocols, and escalation procedures. Regular training and simulations help prepare teams for effective response. The process should focus on speed and efficiency, minimizing the impact on systems and sensitive data. A thorough post-incident analysis is critical, revealing vulnerabilities and informing improvements to security measures, a constant cycle of improvement and adaptation. Failure to act decisively and strategically can have devastating consequences.

Digital forensics plays an increasingly vital role in cybercrime investigations. This specialized field involves the preservation, identification, extraction, documentation, and interpretation of digital evidence. Investigators employ a range of tools and techniques to analyze data from various sources, including computers, mobile devices, and cloud storage. Proper procedures are paramount, ensuring the chain of custody is maintained and evidence is admissible in court. This methodical approach is essential for building a strong legal case, ensuring the integrity and reliability of digital evidence. The ability to analyze complex datasets is vital, requiring a combination of technical skills and legal acumen. Accuracy and attention to detail are paramount, every action is scrutinized, as the evidence will stand or fall on the rigor of the investigation.

7.1 Cybercrime Laws

Understanding cybercrime laws is crucial for anyone involved in the digital world, whether as a user, a developer, or an investigator. These laws are complex and constantly evolving, reflecting the rapid pace of technological innovation and the equally rapid adaptation of criminal activity. Navigating this legal landscape requires a grasp of both the specific statutes and the underlying principles they embody. Jurisdictions differ significantly in their approach to cybercrime, making international cooperation and harmonization of laws a challenging but vital task. However, certain core principles tend to recur across national legal frameworks, providing a common foundation for understanding.

The challenge lies in applying established legal concepts to a new environment. Traditional criminal law often struggles to adapt to the fluid and borderless nature of cyberspace. For example, establishing jurisdiction can be difficult when the perpetrator is in one country and the victim is in another. The question of which legal system applies becomes paramount, a logistical puzzle that lawyers and law enforcement agencies constantly grapple with. The internet's inherent interconnectedness complicates things further. A cyberattack originating in one nation might affect thousands of users across the globe.

One critical area is the definition of "cybercrime" itself. This is not always straightforward, as many actions fall into a gray area, blurring the lines between acceptable behavior and illegal activity. For example, accessing a computer system without authorization might be considered a crime in some instances but acceptable in others, such as penetration testing with proper consent. These legal nuances necessitate careful interpretation and understanding of the context of each specific event. The intent behind the action is crucial, as is evidence of harm or potential harm caused.

Many countries have enacted specific laws targeting cybercrime, often encompassing a wide range of activities. These statutes frequently address offenses such as unauthorized access to computer systems, data theft, malware distribution, and online fraud. Penalties can vary greatly depending on the severity of the crime and the jurisdiction. Some jurisdictions focus on the act itself, whereas others concentrate on the resulting harm. Understanding the specific language of these laws is essential to navigate potential legal issues. This necessitates familiarity with legal terminology and interpretation, often requiring expert legal counsel.

The digital environment presents unique challenges for gathering and presenting evidence. Data is often ephemeral and easily altered or destroyed. This necessitates advanced digital forensics techniques to preserve and analyze evidence. Chain of custody protocols must be meticulously followed to ensure the admissibility of digital evidence in court. Furthermore, international collaboration is frequently needed to acquire evidence stored on servers located in other countries, which presents a significant logistical challenge.

Data protection laws are increasingly important in the context of cybercrime. Regulations such as GDPR in Europe and CCPA in California emphasize the need for organizations to protect personal data. Breaches of these laws can result in significant fines and reputational damage, making it paramount for organizations to implement robust data protection measures. These laws are also relevant in cybercrime investigations, as they often dictate the legal parameters of data access and use during investigations. The complex interplay between data protection laws and cybercrime investigations highlights the need for careful consideration and expert advice.

Understanding the legal landscape of cybercrime is an ongoing process, requiring continuous monitoring of legal developments, both domestically and internationally. The rapid evolution of technology necessitates constant updates to the legal framework, attempting to keep pace with the ever-changing nature of cyber threats. The need for continuous learning and adaptation underlines the importance of staying current with legal updates and seeking expert legal counsel when navigating complex situations. The legal challenges in this domain are dynamic and multifaceted; effective engagement demands ongoing attention and informed decision-making. This chapter serves as a foundation, providing a starting point in this vital but complex field.

7.2 Ethical Hacking

Ethical hacking, often called penetration testing, is a crucial defensive strategy in the ongoing battle against cybercrime. It involves simulating real-world attacks to identify vulnerabilities before malicious actors can exploit them. Unlike malicious hackers who aim to cause damage, ethical hackers operate within a legal and ethical framework, using their skills to strengthen cybersecurity defenses. Their work is vital for organizations of all sizes, safeguarding sensitive data and preventing costly breaches.

The process typically starts with a thorough understanding of the target system. Ethical hackers meticulously map the network infrastructure, identifying potential entry points and weaknesses in security protocols. They might analyze firewalls, intrusion detection systems, and web applications, searching for vulnerabilities that could be leveraged for unauthorized access. This phase involves extensive research, often employing automated tools to scan for common flaws but also relying on manual inspection for more subtle weaknesses. Understanding the architecture and the way the different components communicate is key to anticipating where the weak points could be.

Once the initial assessment is complete, the ethical hacker begins the penetration testing phase. This involves attempting to breach the system's security using various techniques, mirroring the tactics of real-world attackers. This might include exploiting known vulnerabilities in software, attempting social engineering attacks to trick employees into revealing sensitive information, or employing brute-force methods to crack passwords. The goal isn't to cause harm, but to demonstrate the system's vulnerabilities and provide concrete recommendations for improvement. They meticulously document each step, providing detailed reports highlighting vulnerabilities and suggesting remediation strategies.

The critical difference between ethical hacking and malicious hacking lies in authorization and intent. Ethical hackers have explicit permission from the system owner to conduct their activities, ensuring their actions remain within legal bounds. Their goal is not to steal data or disrupt services; instead, they aim to identify weaknesses and help organizations bolster their security postures. Malicious hackers, on the other hand, operate without permission, with the intent to cause harm or gain unauthorized access for personal gain. The legal consequences for malicious activities are severe, involving hefty fines and potentially imprisonment.

A successful ethical hacking engagement results in a comprehensive report detailing identified vulnerabilities, their severity, and recommended solutions. This report is invaluable to organizations, enabling them to prioritize security improvements and allocate resources effectively. This proactive approach to security is far more cost-effective than reacting to a breach after it has occurred. The detailed nature of the findings allows for pinpoint remediation efforts and ensures that specific vulnerabilities can be addressed appropriately, unlike a generic software patch that addresses multiple vulnerabilities at once, which may affect system performance.

Moreover, ethical hacking provides invaluable training for security teams. By simulating real-world attacks, ethical hackers help security personnel understand how attackers think and operate. This hands-on experience enhances their skills in threat detection and response, leading to a more robust and resilient security posture. The involvement of the security teams in the process ensures that the organization's expertise is leveraged and that the suggested remediation strategies are feasible and implemented correctly. The involvement of the security teams in the process ensures that the suggested remediation strategies are feasible and implemented correctly.

Finally, ethical hacking plays a crucial role in compliance with industry standards and regulations. Many industries, such as finance and healthcare, have stringent security requirements. Regular penetration testing demonstrates an organization's commitment to data security and helps them meet regulatory compliance standards. This proactive approach minimizes the risk of non-compliance penalties, which can be far more costly than the investment in ethical hacking services. It also boosts an organization's reputation and instills confidence in its customers and stakeholders.

In conclusion, ethical hacking is a proactive and essential component of a comprehensive cybersecurity strategy. By simulating real-world attacks within a legal and ethical framework, ethical hackers help organizations identify and mitigate vulnerabilities before they can be exploited by malicious actors. Their expertise is invaluable for strengthening security defenses, improving incident response capabilities, and ensuring regulatory compliance. Investing in ethical hacking services is not simply a cost, but a strategic investment in protecting valuable assets and maintaining a strong reputation in today's increasingly complex digital landscape. The knowledge and understanding that come out of a penetration testing exercise can make the difference between an organization staying in business or suffering financial and reputational ruin.

7.3 Data Privacy

Protecting personal data in the digital age is paramount, a complex task demanding a multi-pronged approach. Individuals and organizations alike face unprecedented challenges as data breaches become increasingly sophisticated and frequent. Understanding the various threats and implementing robust preventative measures are crucial steps in mitigating risk. The careless handling of personal information, such as passwords, banking details, or medical records, can have devastating consequences, ranging from financial loss to identity theft and reputational damage. Therefore, proactively securing your data should be a priority.

Unlike previous chapters focusing on the technical aspects of cybercrime, this chapter delves into the human element of data protection. While strong encryption and secure networks are vital, the human factor often represents the weakest link. Phishing emails, cleverly disguised malware, and social engineering tactics successfully exploit human vulnerabilities, gaining access to sensitive data despite technical safeguards. Remember, a robust security system needs to account for human behavior; it's not just about technology, it's also about education.

We must therefore prioritize user education. It's not enough to simply implement sophisticated security systems; users must understand the risks and the importance of their roles in data protection. Companies need to invest in training programs that educate employees on identifying and avoiding phishing scams, recognizing malicious software, and creating strong, unique passwords. Regular security awareness training should be a standard operating procedure, a continuous process rather than a one-off event. The investment in such programs far outweighs the potential costs of data breaches.

For individuals, adopting a proactive approach is key. This involves understanding and implementing basic cybersecurity practices. Using strong and unique passwords, enabling two-factor authentication wherever possible, and regularly updating software are simple yet effective measures. Being cautious about clicking on suspicious links or opening attachments from unknown senders is also crucial. Think before you click; if it seems too good to be true, it probably is. Hesitation is your first line of defense.

Beyond individual actions, legislative frameworks play a critical role. Data privacy laws, such as GDPR and CCPA, aim to provide individuals with more control over their personal data. Understanding the rights granted under these laws empowers individuals to protect their privacy. The right to access, rectify, and erase personal data are essential provisions that help individuals maintain control over their information. Organizations must comply with these regulations to avoid hefty fines and reputational damage.

However, laws alone are not enough; ethical considerations are equally important. Organizations must adopt a privacy-by-design approach, integrating data protection into the design and development process of systems and applications. This involves minimizing data collection, using data only for its intended purpose, and implementing robust security measures to protect data throughout its lifecycle. Transparency and accountability are vital, ensuring that individuals are informed about how their data is collected, used, and protected.

The responsible handling of personal data involves a complex interplay of technological solutions, individual awareness, and robust legal frameworks. While technology provides the tools, user education is the cornerstone of effective data protection. Remember, data is a valuable asset, and protecting it requires a collective effort. By understanding the risks and implementing appropriate measures, both individuals and organizations can significantly reduce their vulnerability to data breaches and safeguard their valuable information.

Negligence is not an option in today's interconnected world. Your vigilance is your shield against digital threats. The cost of inaction far exceeds the cost of preparedness.

7.4 Incident Response

Effective incident response hinges on preparedness. A well-defined incident response plan, regularly tested and updated, is your first line of defense. This plan shouldn't be a dusty document gathering virtual cobwebs; it needs to be a living, breathing document, reflecting the ever-evolving landscape of cyber threats and your organization's specific vulnerabilities. Regular drills, involving key personnel, are crucial to ensure everyone understands their roles and responsibilities in a real-world scenario. This proactive approach dramatically reduces the time it takes to contain and mitigate the damage. Consider including scenarios that simulate various attack vectors, from phishing emails to ransomware attacks, to thoroughly prepare your team. This comprehensive approach will build confidence and competence in dealing with various incidents.

The initial stages of an incident are critical, demanding a swift and decisive response. Time is of the essence; rapid containment minimizes the potential damage. Your plan must outline clear procedures for identifying, isolating, and analyzing compromised systems. This includes isolating affected devices from the network to prevent further spread of malware or unauthorized access. The emphasis should be on containing the breach, preventing its escalation. Effective containment demands a keen understanding of network architecture and system configurations. You need a system for quickly identifying the affected resources and understanding the scope of the damage—establishing a clear chain of custody is crucial for any subsequent legal or forensic investigations. This step ensures you are not destroying any evidence that could be crucial in a later investigation.

Once the immediate threat is contained, a thorough investigation is necessary. This involves identifying the root cause of the incident, determining how the attackers gained access, and assessing the extent of the damage. Detailed logging and monitoring are invaluable tools during this phase. Analyzing system logs, network traffic, and security alerts can provide crucial clues about the attack's origins, methods, and objectives. Remember, meticulous record-keeping is paramount; it forms the foundation of your incident report and assists any subsequent legal proceedings. A clear timeline of events should be established. Use the data collected to build a strong case for any potential prosecutions. This detailed forensic analysis is vital for understanding the overall extent of the compromise and potential long-term effects.

Remediation follows the investigation. This phase focuses on restoring systems to their pre-incident state and implementing measures to prevent similar incidents in the future. This might involve patching vulnerabilities, reinstalling software, and strengthening security protocols. This step requires a thorough understanding of system administration and security best practices. Vulnerability scanning and penetration testing can highlight weaknesses that need addressing. Your aim is to remove the threat, secure the impacted systems, and create a more resilient system that is less susceptible to similar incidents in the future. The more thorough you are in this step, the less likely you are to be victimized by the same attack twice.

Post-incident activity is equally crucial. This includes documenting the entire incident response process, analyzing lessons learned, and updating the incident response plan accordingly. A comprehensive post-incident report should summarize the incident's timeline, root cause analysis, containment strategies, remediation steps, and lessons learned. This should be disseminated within the organization to increase overall security awareness and ensure improved preparedness for future incidents. Regular review and updating of the incident response plan is essential, factoring in the learnings derived from each incident—turning experience into lasting improvements. This continuous improvement cycle strengthens your organization's overall security posture and helps prevent future incidents. It's a cycle of learning, adapting, and improving. Finally, remember the human element; ensure your team receives the appropriate support and training. This includes psychological support, if necessary, and regular training sessions to maintain and sharpen their skills. Investing in your team builds a resilient and responsive incident response capability, fostering a strong security culture within the organization. Through consistent training and continuous learning, the organization enhances its security posture and improves its ability to handle a variety of cyber threats efficiently and effectively.

7.5 Digital Forensics

Digital forensics is the application of computer science and investigative techniques to gather evidence from digital devices. It's a crucial part of cybercrime investigations, helping law enforcement and private entities reconstruct events, identify perpetrators, and build strong cases. Understanding the process, even at a basic level, is invaluable in the fight against cybercrime.

This field isn't just about finding incriminating files; it involves a meticulous, systematic approach to ensure evidence's integrity and admissibility in court. Every step, from securing the scene to analyzing the data, requires precision and documentation. The slightest misstep can compromise an entire investigation. Think of it like a complex puzzle; every piece, no matter how small, contributes to the complete picture.

One of the first steps in any digital forensic investigation is securing the crime scene. This prevents further data loss or alteration, which could severely weaken any later analysis. This isn't merely about physically isolating the device; it includes creating a forensic image—an exact bit-by-bit copy—of the device's storage medium. The original device remains untouched, serving as a backup in case something goes wrong with the image. This ensures the integrity of evidence and prevents accidental or malicious data modification.

After securing the evidence, the forensic examiner begins the process of data acquisition and analysis. This involves using specialized software tools to examine the contents of the forensic image. The tools allow for the recovery of deleted files, the extraction of metadata, and the identification of suspicious network activity. These tools aren't magic wands; skilled interpretation is essential to accurately identify relevant information. The level of expertise required ranges from understanding basic file systems to proficiency in more complex areas like network traffic analysis.

The analysis phase is often time-consuming and requires specific knowledge. The examiner might sift through gigabytes, or even terabytes, of data to find specific pieces of information. They look for things like timestamps, log files, browser history, and deleted communications, all of which can help piece together the sequence of events and potentially identify the culprits. This process requires a keen eye for detail and an understanding of the various ways criminals try to conceal their activities.

Data recovery is a significant component of digital forensics. Even if a file has been deleted, its remnants often remain on the storage medium. Specialized techniques and software can recover this data, allowing investigators to access information the perpetrator might have believed was irretrievably lost. This underscores the importance of properly deleting data; simple deletion is rarely sufficient to ensure data is truly unrecoverable. Secure deletion methods are essential for protecting sensitive information.

The final stage involves reporting. The findings of the investigation must be clearly documented and presented in a way that is understandable to both technical and non-technical audiences. This often involves creating detailed reports, providing expert testimony in court, and explaining complex technical concepts in a clear and concise manner. The credibility of the forensic examiner is paramount; the accuracy and integrity of the report are directly linked to the strength of the case. Therefore, comprehensive documentation is absolutely essential, including a complete chain of custody and a detailed methodology section.

Beyond the technical aspects, ethical considerations are equally important. Digital forensics involves handling sensitive personal information, and strict adherence to privacy laws and ethical guidelines is crucial. Forensic examiners must be mindful of their responsibilities and act with integrity throughout the investigative process, ensuring that their actions are lawful and respect individual rights. This underscores the vital link between digital forensics and legal considerations, demonstrating the need for a balanced approach to both technical skill and ethical awareness.

Therefore, digital forensics involves more than just technical prowess. It's a blend of technical expertise, investigative skills, and ethical awareness, requiring a thorough understanding of both computer science and legal procedures. For those interested in entering this field, it requires continuous learning and adaptation as cybercrime techniques constantly evolve. The role of a digital forensic examiner is pivotal in combating cybercrime and bringing criminals to justice; it is a field that demands both technical proficiency and dedication to justice. By mastering the intricacies of this field, professionals can contribute significantly to the fight against online fraud and deception. It demands a dedication to detail and a commitment to upholding the principles of justice. The field is constantly evolving, demanding continuous learning and adaptation.

www.ingramcontent.com/pod-product-compliance
Lightning Source LLC
LaVergne TN
LVHW022018200926
848481LV00007B/2448